# My name is Gretchen

*A   MEMOIR*

My favorite childhood cousin was my birth mother

an adoption secret revealed

Gretchen L. vanHoosier

CONNECTICUT
RIVER PRESS

Published by Connecticut River Press

First edition, August 2004

ISBN 0-9706573-4-X

Library of Congress Control Number 2004093622

To order *My name is Gretchen* directly from the publisher
(hardcover, $27.95 + $5.00 shipping/handling—includes sales tax):

Connecticut River Press
111 Holmes Road, Dept. A
Newington, CT 06111
(860) 666-0615
(860) 666-0535 fax
Order toll-free with your Visa/MasterCard (800) 803-9551

For more information about *My name is Gretchen* and the author,
visit her website at www.gretchenvanhoosiercollections.com.

## DEDICATION

*This book is respectfully dedicated with love to those in my maternal clan who named me and kept me in the family—the late Rose Hartley Nipps (my grandmother); her daughter, the late Louise Nipps Martin (my favorite Aunt Weese); her daughter, Virginia Martin Beasley (my favorite childhood cousin Gingie, my birth mother); and my grandmother's daughter, the late Wilma Nipps Van Hoosier (Louise's sister, Gingie's aunt, my mother)—and to the late Everett Lee Van Hoosier (my beloved father), "Who went along with it," as my mother told me so many times.*

## TRIBUTE

*This book literally came into being because Gail Champlin, my friend, and her mother, Jean Champlin, made it possible with their loving encouragement and support—including the financial wind beneath my wings. Their caring can be found on every page and I am forever grateful.*

A portion of the proceeds from this book will go to The Florence Crittenton School in Denver, Colorado, originally founded in 1893 as a residential home for unwed mothers—to continue to help pregnant teenagers with a wide range of services. My beloved birth mother was one of those young teenagers when I was born back in 1937.

# C O N T E N T S

*(continued)*

# CONTENTS

"Making your unknown known—"

Georgia O'Keeffe

This book has been a long and longing process of peeling away the layers to my past, literally and emotionally—and at the same time, writing about it. It took as long as it took for me to come to the truth of where I came from.

My words speak for me, how it was for me, "Growing Up" and "Finding Out." I have not meant to speak for others, unless I have said so. However, at times I have had to conjecture to fill in between the lines of what I know—to try to understand how it must have been for the others in what they had to go through. I do know that only they could have spoken the truth for themselves, only they knew for sure how it was for them. Then their words would have been their stories.

Even though some of my family have passed away and some are still here, I have written my stories in the past tense to cast my book in the past, where it came from.

Throughout my writing, my mother and my birth mother most enthusiastically cheered me on with my book—those same two women who would have taken the secret to their graves, had I not persevered. I am forever grateful that the truth came to light while we could all share it together.

I feel blessed by my family that my mother and my cousin/birth mother Gingie and my cousin Bam all gave me photographs that could be with my words in this book.

I honor that child within that didn't give up, that didn't take no for an answer—her light prevailed. That said, here is my story.

# PART ONE: GROWING UP

My big brother Jan was sitting close to me, his newly arrived baby sister Gretchen.
That was my basket.

My Mother Told Me

My name is Gretchen and I was adopted. I know that because my mother told me so when I was a little girl. I remember standing by that big old green ironer in the kitchen where she was ironing white sheets to make them flat and smooth for our beds. She said they wanted a little girl and they picked me out special.

Her telling me told me I was different. In that moment I suddenly felt different, that I was different from everyone else in my family, and somehow not as good as my brothers. No doubt to assure me, my mother said a neighbor boy was also adopted. Even a little girl could feel relief. That meant there were two of us in the world like that and I wasn't all alone.

And even though she told me in a loving way, I could tell it was a subject not to be discussed. Somehow what she told me had a period at the end of it.

In looking back, I can appreciate how that moment must have hung over her, of how and when she would tell me that I was adopted. It must have been hard to know what to say so as not to say too much. And how many times had she rehearsed it over and over in her mind?

Eventually I realized that the secret of who I was couldn't even be known by me—I had to be kept a secret from myself.

A Place Called Home

I grew up in a place called home. I always belonged to that place where my family had drawn a circle that included me. Home was knowing it was there for me, that I could count on it and it wouldn't go away.

MotherandDaddy—those words rolled off my tongue like one word—they had a way of being inseparable, they went together. Mother was the dominant presence in our family, but she counted on Daddy backing her up. For any differences they had, there was an abiding love between them that ran deep and got them through hard times. Whatever happened, we were a family—with a mother and a father and three children and our grandmother next-door. I had two brothers and I was between them in ages. My big brother Jan was six years older than me, and my little brother Michael was two years younger. Sometimes I squabbled with my brothers, but it never lasted long before we were back together again.

My parents had bought our house from my mother's parents, my maternal grandparents, after they built a smaller one next-door. We called our place 120—it wasn't the street address that made the difference, it was that sense of place where we belonged—and our grandmother was next-door at 130.

We lived out beyond the city limits—with lots of wide open spaces that went all the way to the mountains, and an open sky all around. Our street was short and quiet. Some of it was gravel which was good for riding my horse, but bumpy for riding my bicycle. I rode my bicycle on the smooth pavement part. I knew all the neighbors and they knew me. I could count on them being where they belonged.

There was an inviting old climbing tree on the north side of our house—it had a swing that took me high into the sky, and I would climb up in the branches to be alone up there. I liked to tuck into hiding places that were mine.

Our place was where relatives liked to gather for summer picnics in our backyard—the men-folk played horseshoes, and the children played badminton and croquet and went barefoot in the grass. In the summers there were old-fashioned pink hollyhocks that bloomed near the back door. No one tended to them, they just tended to themselves.

I loved my bedroom. It was my very own and I decided how it would be. At night I would snuggle into my bed and listen to the train whistles far off in the distance and wonder where they were going. In the morning I woke up to be greeted by the sun shining on my mountains out my window. My favorite childhood book was "Heidi" and she had mountains out her window, too.

We had a front porch and the local dairy delivered milk right to our front door early in the morning—the milkman put the bottles in a little wooden box. I remember the cold glass bottles with cardboard lids and how when we first opened them we poured that heavy cream off the top.

The native stone fireplace in the living room was the heart of our home at 120. Whenever it was cold enough to have a fire, we would watch the flames dancing about and feel the warmth that reached those places that needed warming.

There were times when we had to move away from home because of Daddy's work. Whenever we were away from 120, renters would be there, living in those private places that were mine. I tried not to think about it. And I was away from my grandmother. Being away from home was like being in a holding pattern in an airplane, waiting until you could land where you belonged.

Our family all together—Mother and Daddy with their three children Jan and Gretchen and Michael. We were dressed up from going somewhere.

My Mother's Ways

It wasn't easy for my mother and me as I was growing up. We clashed sometimes, and that was hard for both of us. We also had times of closeness over the years and that was what mattered.

Even though I was adopted, my mother was my mother and her ways made what she did special to her daughter.

She made jars of crabapple jelly from our very own crabapple trees and sealed them with her love and layers of wax so they would keep.

She baked her apple crisp and made smooth prune whip and said, "My, my Junket is nice," while she stirred it on the stove.

She knew when I was hurting inside and she knew when she couldn't make it all better, however hard she might try.

She sewed merit badges on my Girl Scout uniform when I earned them.

She sat proudly with the other mothers at my piano recitals.

She wrapped me in a blanket in the warm winter sun on the patio when I was sick, and made me tomato soup with milk.

She wanted me to have what I wanted and it hurt her when she had to say no.

She loved her books and reading and she shared that world with me.

She made sure my favorite orange plate was on the table at my place to eat.

She had a delightful sense of humor when she let it show.

Mother planted flowers in her garden that bloomed for all of us. They were always Mother's flowers, even though Daddy did the hard work. She would wander among her flowers early on a summer morning to see how they were doing—and I knew they were always doing better because she was with them.

My mother was not so strong of body because of poor health most of her life. She suffered from heart problems that caused her to have to take it easy and often lay low. Mother attended to her domestic responsibilities with a lot of help from Daddy. But her spirit was strong, particularly when it came to who and what she loved. Mother mostly loved her family and her home and she was very proud of her children—her light would come shining through my brothers and me.

She knew to have angels on the mantle, even past Christmas. Each year several of them lingered after Mother's Christmas collection of angels had been carefully packed away until next year.

My mother was a proud woman. She was a tall woman and carried herself with dignity. Some might even say she was like her father in that she could be somewhat aloof at times. Perhaps that protected whatever was inside her that needed to be protected. She had a definite presence about her when she was photographed.

My mother could be very opinionated and critical of others, including me. She could be outspoken or withhold comment. Sometimes it wasn't what she said but what she didn't say that said it all. I don't like to think of her being that way. She also had a sweetness about her that went right to my heart.

My mother was always there for me—I could count on her being there. It took time for me to know that my mother was what I needed her to be—for me to be Gretchen, to be influenced by her.

I wanted to be like the part of my mother that longed for what she couldn't reach in the stars. I wanted to join her on that path that pondered the meaning of a poem, rather than discussing what was on her grocery list. Now I know that she taught me to dream dreams and follow them.

My Father's Ways

My father was a gentle man, quiet, and soft-spoken—and it was his way to take care
of his family above all else.
He went about doing what needed to be done, for us and for Grandmother next-
door, and others if they needed him.
He was down to earth and practical and knew how to fix most anything—I figured
he was born knowing about such things. Though he had experience in many fields,
Daddy was known for his expertise in electronics.
Daddy was a man of few words—sometimes I wasn't sure what he was thinking
about me—so when he said something, his words counted and I listened.
Whenever he called me Honey-child I felt all warm inside.

Daddy took life in stride most of the time. He had patience and a dignity about
him. He was an honest man. He had a way of accepting things the way they were.
He generally didn't reach beyond his grasp. He had a wisdom of knowing that he
couldn't change what he couldn't change—he just let it be.

Everything Daddy did he took care in the doing of it, with a sense of pride. I like to
think some of that rubbed off on his daughter.

Daddy made tremendous sacrifices for his family—like when he lived all alone in an
apartment in Denver because of his work, coming home to Colorado Springs only
on weekends until the distance and separation got to be too much for all of us.

He loved to go fishing, to be off alone along a mountain stream in Colorado, and it
didn't much matter to him if he caught any fish. When I was a little girl, sometimes
he would let me go with him to the bank of a stream where we were camping in the
mountains—to be close to his fishing was to be close to him. I saw his light shining
in him at times like that.

When I was growing up, I longed for a private place where nobody could get in
unless I let them. Daddy found that space for me—it was a small side room in the

9

garage and it had its own door, and he put a padlock on it with a key just for me. It was all mine. I felt so snug and safe all tucked in there with the sun shining through the only window. That's where I kept my favorite things hidden. Sometimes I would let others in. I called it my Clubhouse so it sounded secluded and private. Of course it was misnamed since a club denotes members and I was the only self-appointed member of that sacred space.

Daddy had a hard time letting go if someone did something against him—like how he was treated at work sometimes. His holding a grudge didn't seem to fit his kind nature, but it was a part of him. It's hard for me to say that.

I was my father's daughter when it came to gravy. We would make deep holes in our mountains of mashed potatoes to hold the gravy—then pour the gravy until it overflowed down the sides of the potatoes onto our plates. Now I know that gravy gave comfort in deep places for Daddy and me.

When asked how he was, Daddy often replied, "Right-side-up-with-care."

Whenever a problem would arise with something he was doing, Daddy would say, "Whose idea was this?" or "What we need is a sky hook." A sky hook is akin to Santa Claus and I believe in both of them.

I had a blue bicycle. I would ride my bike up to the corner and down a dirt path to meet Daddy when he got off the bus from work—and then we went home together.

The children of our family were at home at 120—Michael and me, with Jan on his bicycle. That was where we all belonged.

My Big Brother Jan

My big brother Jan was older than me and I looked up to him all my life, regardless of the years that passed. He was always my big brother—he was there to greet me when his family became my family, too.

My big brother was the one who taught me how to ride a bicycle when I got big enough. His lesson was basic—he told me how to ride while helping me up on the seat perched high on his big bicycle. My shoes barely reached the pedals, and he assured me that once he gave me a push, I would stay upright! He was right! I had suddenly learned how to ride a bicycle—until it came time to stop and I couldn't remember what to do. It was a big boy's bicycle with a bar across from the seat so I couldn't just swing my short leg over and jump off. So I leaned to the side and gravity took over and we came to a stop on the gravel road. That was when I learned that starting and stopping go together, and to remember that!

Both my brothers were always tinkering with mechanical things with Daddy, things that didn't interest me even a little bit. They seemed to have games of taking things apart and putting them back together again, only better. Or so they said.

My big brother Jan had a go-cart that he drove around and around on a small track that he made on our property. I wanted to drive it, too, just because it was so important to him. At least he let me sit in it!

Jan had an endearing look about his face when he was a little boy—I have seen it in the photographs in the family albums—and when we were growing up it would sometimes show and warm the hearts of those who saw it. That was my big brother.

My Little Brother Michael

My little brother Michael never caught up to me, no matter how old he got. He was just two years younger than me so we ended up doing things together more than with our older brother Jan.

I called my little brother Butch. I knew his real name was Michael, but I came up with my own nickname for him. I don't know where it came from. I think he liked it—it was something special just between us.

He must have been 9 or 10 when he handmade a little blue-and-white sailboat and took it with him when we went to California one summer. I thought he was so smart, the way he knew how to set the sails when he put it in the water in that small lake—and then he would run around to the other side of the lake to meet it when it came ashore.

Butch and I loved to go to Aunt Weese and Uncle Tom's house for overnight on weekends. We would fill our trays with food and set up wobbly tv tables, parking ourselves in front of those early black-and-white years of television.

My little brother Michael was born on Valentine's Day, and Mother always made him a cake in the shape of a heart. As a child, I wished that my birthday had a shape that could be made into a cake.

Butch had a hard time when he had to stay in bed for a year with rheumatic fever at an age when little boys were called out to play. I would go home after school and sit on his bed and play games with him. Who knows what dreams began in him during that time of getting well.

Grandfather and Grandmother Nipps, my maternal grandparents, with their
grown-up children—Uncle Herbert (left) and Uncle Hartley, and back row (l to r)
my mother Wilma, Aunt Reba, Aunt Lowell, and Aunt Louise (Weese).

My Maternal Grandparents

My maternal grandparents and their four daughters migrated from Missouri in 1911—to file on a homestead north of the tiny town of Eads, out on the desolate eastern plains of Colorado. Their first son was born there.

Grandfather Nipps was a dentist and he had also built a large business building in town, the first of its kind there. By all accounts, Dr. William H. Nipps was a most prominent citizen in Eads back then, and he basked in it for the rest of his life—to the point that he continued to spend most of his time out in Eads, even after his family settled in Colorado Springs.

Although her husband was insistent on making a fine school system in Eads, Grandmother couldn't wait. It was Grandmother who went against her husband's wishes and set out alone with their children, to find them a good education. Like the pioneering woman that she was, she went west—first to the town of Pueblo, where the mountains could be seen—and then to the foothills of those mountains, to the town of Colorado Springs. She eventually found Cheyenne Mountain School and they settled in that school district. They rented at first, before Grandfather Nipps bought property and had a house built in walking distance to the school.

From then on, my maternal grandparents spent most of their married life in two separate places. So much so that I don't have memories of my Grandfather Nipps. In fact, it was always called Grandmother's place, next door to us, when any of the relatives identified where Grandmother lived.

Grandfather Nipps lived in Eads mostly. They got together for short periods over the years—and their youngest son was born in Colorado Springs. But it was Grandmother who was steady as a rock and made a home for their children and was there for them when they needed her.

Four cousins with Grandmother—Sharon in her lap and me close beside her. The double cousins (their mothers married two brothers) Bam (left) and Gingie were standing behind Grandmother, the matriarch of our family.

My Grandmother Next-Door

My maternal grandmother lived next-door to us, alone without her husband most of the time. He stayed out on the prairie in Eads. They both made choices that kept them apart the majority of their married life.

Grandmother raised their children, while her husband attended to other matters. You might even say that my grandmother wore the pants in her family, though I never saw her in pants. She was always in dresses—simple cotton prints for everyday and more dressed-up ones for church or company coming or whatever came along that called for a change of clothes.

My grandmother was practical and wasn't wasteful. She had a sense of humor that would sneak up on you unexpected. She also had comments to make about politicians. Grandmother could be critical of members of her family, but would staunchly defend the same ones if anyone on the outside said anything—she protected her own like a mother hen. Most of all, she had a simple basic faith in God. She was our sweet little grandmother. More accurately, she was our strong and tenacious grandmother.

When I stayed overnight at Grandmother's, I would snuggle down safe in her featherbed with her and listen to the coyotes howling out on the foothills behind the house. Such sounds made me sure I was safe and where I belonged.

If I had problems at home, like with my mother, I went next-door to get Grandmother to side with me. Although she never took sides against her own daughter, she would patiently listen to me and then say, "That's the way she is." Grandmother was right and everything felt right again with me and my mother.

There was a well-worn path between our house and Grandmother's next-door— across a narrow little footbridge that Daddy built to span that dry creek bed. The creek had water in it only when those sudden summer downpours came rushing down from the foothills. Sometimes the creek flooded its banks and overflowed onto Grandmother's lawn—and made a small lake to splash around in barefooted! Nature came calling with all kinds of surprises for little children.

My grandmother had chickens out back, beyond her vegetable garden. She loved her chickens and they knew it. Often I tagged along when she went to feed them. Whenever we walked through the fence gate into their pen, Grandmother's chickens came running toward her, clucking all around her feet as she scattered the cracked corn on the ground with her big farm hands. Her chickens had a house with roosts to sleep on at night and soft straw nests for laying their eggs—sometimes the eggs were still warm when we went to gather them in the basket. And every night, Grandmother would go out to the chicken house to tell them goodnight and close the door so nothing could harm them. In the spring, Grandmother would buy just-hatched baby chicks down at the feed store and set them up in a box in her attic with a lightbulb hanging down to keep them warm—and she would let me climb up the handmade ladder and stand on the top step to see them peeping in the box.

Grandmother kept sticks of doublemint chewing gum in a kitchen cabinet drawer that was higher than I could reach, even on tiptoes. When I went next-door to be with my grandmother, she would hand me down a stick of that green-wrapper gum. It was a ritual of our being together, and the same gum wouldn't have been the same anywhere else on earth.

I took my little brother Michael for rides on my horse. There we were at Grandmother's next-door, with big round lollipops that someone had brought us.

Night Driving to Kansas

I remember riding in the backseat of our '39 Ford with my little brother Michael—
driving at night across the plains of eastern Colorado and into Kansas where our
paternal grandparents lived on a farm.

Daddy was driving and Mother had to keep fiddling with the car radio, trying to
get a station that would stay with us for more than a few miles. Back then you
couldn't choose much what you listened to. But we were content just to have some
contact with the world in all that darkness as we drove along—often the only car for
long stretches on those narrow two-lane roads that linked rural America from town
to town. It was amazing how we could pull in radio stations from as far away as
Texas, and yet not be able to hold one from a nearby town.

It was so dark as we bumped along in the night that we could see the distant glow
of each little town as we approached it—even with the sky so full of stars you could
pluck them for keeps.

One of our trips to Kansas to visit our paternal grandparents on their farm. Grandmother Van was holding me. Jan looked so proud in his stylish knickers and high boots. There must have been two photographers that day.

My Paternal Grandparents

My paternal grandparents had a farm in Kansas when I was growing up. They were farmers and lived close to the land in every way. To a little girl, that flat farmland stretched out to where the earth curved—and it was planted with crops of wheat and sorghum that had to be harvested with big heavy equipment when the time came. My Grandfather Van told me so.

My father was the firstborn, which was very important in that family. He had only one sibling, my Uncle Arvin, who I knew by name but barely knew in person. It was that way with all of Daddy's relatives, because I saw them only a few times while growing up.

Uncle Arvin lived nearby his parents. He had his own Piper-Cub airplane and he took us up so we could look down on those vast fields of crops and see from the sky where the earth curved. They called it the horizon—the place where the sun came up every morning and went back down every night. It was comforting to count on the sun doing that. It still is.

Whenever I think of my grandparents in Kansas, I remember their breakfasts. After Grandfather Van had gone out to feed the animals and finish the early morning chores on the farm, he was ready for breakfast. And Grandmother Van would have prepared what seemed to be a usual breakfast—you had your choice of bacon and ham and sausage and steak (all four if you wanted) with eggs cooked your way, crispy brown fried potatoes, and big biscuits from scratch with that thick white gravy, or homemade jelly, of course. It was abundance beyond belief as we all gathered around the table together in the name of family.

Our Mountains

I grew up with mountains. They were our mountains and I could count on them being there. They were there, beyond our backyard, ever beckoning to us.

We would go up in the mountains on Sunday afternoon drives, and for family picnics, and on longer trips in the fall to behold the quaking aspen leaves when they turned themselves into gold.

Many of our summer vacations were spent camping in the mountains and sleeping under a sky of stars, with the sounds of a stream nearby. We would claim our campsite in that wilderness and make it ours with our tents and sleeping bags—and gather enough dry wood to get a campfire going for cooking and to be around as a family. The ground could be hard and uneven in the mountains, so you had to pay attention where you put your sleeping bag—before it got dark and you were in it! The trusty flashlight didn't help much then.

One summer when we were camping, I was fascinated by the fireflies out in the night air—turning on and off and on again, lighting up the darkness here and there, so many places I didn't know where to look. Daddy helped me catch some in a jar so I could hold the fireflies in my hands. But they were not themselves that way and I let them go. The magic was having them surprise me in the dark, not knowing when and where they would be.

The mountains were where home was and where we belonged, however farflung life would take us away from them. They still watch over me from afar. They can do that—my mother said so.

Our backyard opened up to the pasture and the foothills and the mountains—and
it always felt like it was all ours, we belonged to it.

Of Fences and Foothills

The horse pasture and foothills were an extension of our own backyard—separated only by an old wire fence that we could crawl through, if we were careful. It was like we had access to all that vastness, it was ours even though it really did belong to somebody else.

It belonged to the Horse Lady—that was my name for her—and she would ride regal around the boundary of her property on her horse, both of them dressed-up in the English attire of riding. I would pat her horses and talk to them when they came by our back fence. When I had my own horse, there in our backyard, her horses would come by and they would visit over the fence. That fence was there to keep her horses in, not to keep us out. We somehow knew we were always welcome to go beyond that back fence.

I loved to go alone into the pasture and walk up into the foothills—cactus was everywhere, so I had to watch my step. Granite rocks hugged the hills, here and there, and provided places for me to sit—I had my favorites that felt so familiar they were like my own. That world was mostly the sky meeting the mountains to the west, and the flat plains to the east—and the sound of a meadowlark singing made it all complete.

Starting in early spring with the rare purplish Pasque flower, my foothills bloomed with wildflowers—and the stately white yucca spires and clumps of red Indian paintbrush and others came in the summertime.

When it got cold and winter was coming, I would go into the pasture to carefully pick a few wild rose hips to carry me into spring, when they would bloom again.

Thank you, dear Horse Lady, for letting us go beyond the fence between us, for letting your land be our land, too.

Little Gretchen loved to be with her Aunt Weese and it showed! That day my little brother Michael was there, too, with his hobbyhorse.

My Favorite Aunt Weese and Uncle Tom

My favorite aunt was Margaret Louise Nipps Martin, my mother's sister closest in age. She was my favorite cousin Gingie's mother. The cousins all called her Aunt Weese. I didn't know where she got that nickname, but she loved it. To everyone else she was Louise, her middle name.

I loved to go visit Aunt Weese and Uncle Tom on weekends, all by myself—just me and my Aunt Weese mostly. They lived at 444—that's what we called their place, without a street name.

I remember Aunt Weese's hands and her fingernails—they were neatly trimmed and simply kept. Her hands made things I loved to eat, and they touched me to tell me that I belonged. Sometimes I thought my hands looked like hers and I liked that.

Aunt Weese would give me a little girl's handful of pennies and off I would go—up the sidewalk a few doors to the corner grocery store. Sometimes I would skip my way there to pick and choose my little-brown-bag of penny candy. Such abundance!

In the summers, Uncle Tom would set up the ice cream maker on the picnic table under the apple tree—he cranked and cranked it with rock salt and elbow grease until it turned to vanilla ice cream. I would hold my bowl of ice cream close to me, feeling held by it.

My favorite photograph of my favorite childhood cousin named Virginia,
nicknamed Gingie. She was so fun-loving and fun to be with.

My Favorite Cousin Gingie

My favorite childhood cousin was Gingie. Her real name was Rose Virginia, named after our maternal grandmother, Rose Hartley Nipps, the matriarch of our family. Gingie, so nicknamed by her mother, was known as Virginia all her life. The name Rose was already taken in our family and it belonged to our beloved grandmother.

Gingie lived in Texas with her husband Sam most of my growing-up years, and she would come home to Colorado Springs for summer vacations. She loved being with her mother.  I loved being with Gingie whenever I could, and her parents, my Aunt Weese and Uncle Tom, would take me with them to meet her train when she came home in the summer. We always had to wait for her luggage—there were big flatbed baggage carts with big wheels and long handles for pulling the suitcases loaded on from the train. We didn't mind waiting—it was so good to be together again.

Those were happy times, when Gingie and I got together. I had her on a pedestal, she was so much older than me. We would go over to nearby Manitou Springs—a small tourist town nestled at the foot of Ute Pass, which was the way to drive up into the mountains, and to Pike's Peak. We were carefree and silly those summers— eating cotton candy and Patsy's popcorn and going in and out of curio shops, buying nearly worthless trinkets that made me feel like I had a million dollars! Being with my favorite cuz', as she called me, turned everything to gold.

Little Gretchen was sitting all sweet with her cousins (l to r) Bam and Gingie and Margaret. I even had a pretty bow in my hair just like Gingie.

My Cousin Bam

My second favorite childhood cousin was Bam. Her real name was Betty Anne Martin and we called her Bam from the initials of her name. Her mother was my Aunt Lowell, my mother's youngest sister.

Bam would be at family gatherings at Grandmother's next-door and picnics in our backyard—and she made me feel good just being around her. She was so sweet and soft-spoken, tall and thin with red hair. My father sometimes called her Carrot Top, but mostly he called her Slim Princess—his most endearing name for his favorite niece. You could tell they were close when they were together. They both had their quiet ways that seemed to understand each other.

I remember when her family moved to Missouri, and then Bam came to live with Grandmother when she got a job in Colorado Springs. She was close to our grandmother and Grandmother was close to her—and I liked to be close to both of them whenever I could.

My Hometown

My hometown was Colorado Springs, Colorado. It was settled in 1871 at the foot of Pike's Peak, on the front range of the Rocky Mountains, with the vast Great Plains stretching out to the east.

We had a main street named Tejon and it ran north and south and that's where the stores were mostly, and the bank. That was where Mother would park the car and my little brother and I were put in charge of putting pennies in the parking meter when it ran out. We also watched passersby come and go on the sidewalk—it was like a stage and we had front row seats. Colorado Springs was a small town back then and even though I didn't know who they were, or their names, it felt like everyone that walked by belonged to me and to each other because we all belonged there in our hometown.

The names of the Ute and Chief movie theaters on Pike's Peak Avenue told the story that our town was settled in territory where others had been before us. We took their native land and called it our native land—but that's another story.

My hometown of Colorado Springs looked like this when I was growing up.
Everybody knew their way around in our small town, and the mountains were the
backdrop to everything we did.

*(Colorado Springs Pioneers Museum, Starsmore Center for Local History)*

There I stood in front—and Mother and Gingie and Sam were in the back. This was our backyard, and Daddy was raising the roof at 120 to make more room for his family.

The Circus Came to Town

It was a big event when the Circus came to town. One year my mother took us to meet the circus train when it arrived, so we could watch them unload the animals.

The air was filled with anticipation and my feet could feel the rumble of the train on the tracks as it got closer and closer. Then it arrived! What a whirlwind of activity it was as the men prepared the ramps for unloading the animals. Mother guided us even closer so we could see the big circus animals when they came off the train one-by-one.

I was so little, the boxcars so big, and the elephants were huge. Men were leading them down the ramps with ropes. Suddenly it wasn't fun for me anymore. Somehow the elephants and I were the same size in spirit when I saw the sweetness in their eyes. I was so sad when I saw the elephants with chains on their feet, all linked together in captivity so they wouldn't run away. Did anyone ask them if they wanted to join the circus to see the world?

Everybody loved the Circus coming to town—except me. I don't remember if we went to the Circus that year. For a sensitive little girl, I did enough remembering.

Tying Shoes and Such

When I was old enough to tie my own shoes, my tie-shoes were stiff brown oxfords. I had a hard time learning how to tie them the way it was supposed to be done. I tried and tried and couldn't get it right. I was all fingers and laces without results. Then I figured out how to tie my shoes on my own—and my shoes always ended up tied like they were supposed to be.

But I still felt funny whenever I had to tie my shoes in front of anyone—because I did it differently and it showed. There it was—one of many lifelong lessons to let go of what others think.

It got so if anyone noticed me tying my shoes, I spoke up immediately and pointed out how I had invented my own way to tie my shoes. Then I couldn't be compared to the right way. What if my way was the right way? It was, for me.

Going to Church

I was a good girl whenever I went to church. Everyone said so. It was where I went to get approval and to get away from disapproval. I wanted to be told I was a good girl. So I got all wrapped up in activities related to church. They said their way was the right way and I didn't want to be wrong. Something deep inside me felt like I wasn't good enough just being Gretchen. I needed to be saved from being Gretchen.

Even though it was where I went to get approval—inside and outside that edifice—those at my childhood church always seemed to be pointing a finger at me to try harder and be better so I would be good enough. And there were authorities everywhere that seemed to be aligned with the church, all pointing fingers at me with that same message.

I never seemed good enough just being Gretchen. It seemed always just beyond my grasp. But still, I was a good girl if I went to church. Everyone said so. And I wanted to be a good girl and get approval.

Perhaps that was more about needing to question authority, than whether a little girl was good enough to get approval.

Our family was on a summer vacation in the mountains—and Michael and I
proudly posed with the catch of the day. We were staying in a rustic log cabin near a
stream where Daddy caught these fish.

Animals for Food

I remember my child's way of not wanting animals to be killed and how it upset me when they were. One time Daddy and my big brother Jan went deer hunting up in the mountains and came home with a deer and hung it in the garage to skin it. I could hardly bear it. I wondered if it was hard for them to shoot the deer. I knew they did it to help put food on our table. We also raised white rabbits and had chickens for food and I suffered through that, too.

And next-door my grandmother would kill one of her beloved old hens when it came time for her to make her family's favorite chicken-and-noodles-from-scratch. I had a way of getting attached to animals when I was a little girl—and I just didn't know how Grandmother could ring their necks or use a hatchet on the tree stump to kill her hens. Was that what pioneer women did? Eventually I decided that her hens gave her permission when she chose each one for such an honored family tradition. My imagination rescued my little girl's sensitive nature more than once.

My little brother Michael was sitting on the running board of our 1936 Plymouth.
This was my family portrait of our trip to California one summer. I took this
picture with my very own Brownie box camera.

California Summer Trips

There were summers in my childhood when we took those long automobile trips from Colorado to California. To try to pass the time and the miles, we played games as we drove along on those endless two-lane roads—like counting license plates on cars from as many different states as possible. Sometimes long lines of freight trains in the distance would be going the same direction we were and we counted the number of boxcars.

One summer on our trip to California, we crossed the desert in the early morning hours when it wouldn't be so hot. When we got to Needles, California, it was 103° at 3:00 in the morning part of night—we even got popsicles when we stopped at the gas station. As children, we had our own version of air-conditioning as we rode along in the backseat of our 1936 Plymouth—we wet washcloths with water and held them up between the open windows and our faces!

I remember one summer in California when I would walk to a nearby park with my dog Freckles, always with a dime stuffed down safe in my pocket for two big nickel ice cream cones on the way—one for me and one for Freckles. Those ice cream cones made our world complete, or was it just being together?

Perhaps it was that same summer when we lived in a little house with a tiny yard, just the right size that was fun for a little girl to take care of—and I did. My finishing touch would be to water the patch of grass and hose down the sidewalk. I loved to play with water that way. It seemed to bless everything, like rain does.

Going away on trips made it feel so good to get home again.

The tradition of Cheyenne Mountain School belonged to our family—and it began for me when Mother took me to school for the first time to this kindergarten building. She was right, there were those who greeted me and made me feel welcome in that unfamiliar world beyond my home.

*(Seedlet to Big Boy—An Impression of Cheyenne Mountain School)*

My School

Cheyenne Mountain School was legendary and those were hallowed halls in our family. The glory had gone before me. My mother had gone to Cheyenne and was close to Pappy and Mrs. Shaw, the visionaries behind what it had become over the years. The history and traditions were there waiting for me when it was time for me to go to that school.

I knew before I knew what it meant that Cheyenne Mountain School was like a shining star to our family and that its light would shine on me, too.

It went way back to when my maternal grandmother found Cheyenne Mountain School so her children would have a good education. Cheyenne School dated back to the 1870s, but the school we knew was built in 1910 and was named for the mountain it was near. The name of "Cheyenne" first came to the area from the native Cheyenne Indians who had their encampments in that region.

I didn't do very well in school, in the ways they gave grades. My grades seemed only average, and I dreaded Report Cards and having to take them home. My potential could be compared to relatives who had gone before me—and I didn't measure up to them or to my classmates back then, in the ways such things were measured.

But there was a spirit about that Cheyenne Mountain School that beckoned to me to find my own light to stand in. That beloved old school had been handed down to me and had become a part of me, too.

When I was nine years old, I was picked to be the star in a school play called
"Polly Patchwork." I was at the center of attention and it made me feel so special.
My mother handmade all of my costumes, and there I was having my picture taken
in one of them—complete with a crisp white pinafore and frilled pantaloons!

My Mother, The Writer

My mother was a writer. Her glory days with her writing were at Cheyenne Mountain School and for several years after she graduated. Lloyd "Pappy" Shaw was an educator and the principal of the school, and Dorothy Stott Shaw was a poet, the school librarian and the head of the high school English Department—they were legends in their own time. The Shaws were Mother's teachers and mentors and she was close to them and took pride in that.

After she was married, Mother was a teacher at Cheyenne, for the senior English class themes, following in the footsteps of Mrs. Shaw—not grading, but helping them grow by reading their themes and writing her notes on them. She even took over editing the "Tyro" literary magazine for Mrs. Shaw.

Cheyenne Mountain School was my mother's touchstone for life—her connection to the Shaws and to Cheyenne connected her to herself. It was my school, too, and Mrs. Shaw had influenced my writing as well. I cherish that connection to Cheyenne and my mother's writing back then.

Mother didn't pursue her writing much after that. She said she once had a literary agent, and then she talked about those dreaded rejection slips that came in the mail.

My mother was a writer and she passed onto me her passion for words. As I was writing this book, she said to me, "I worked so hard to have things published, and all those dreams—now look at my little girl." I'm carrying the torch for both of us.

As an aside—if she really, really agreed with something, my mother would say, "Just so." So I took it to heart whenever she said those words about my writing. It made me feel like I had arrived as a writer in her eyes.

A woman named Marie came to help take care of us when Mother wasn't well—and she was like family to us. Then she had to go off to help with the war. She looked very proud in her uniform and my little brother Michael and I seemed to be standing at attention beside her. She came back safe to us after the war was over.

Bragging Rights and Wrongs

There was a time when I was growing up when marbles were big. I don't remember that it was so much about playing games with them that mattered, as much as collecting them.

I do remember one day at school, it was during recess, that a small gathering of us were bragging about the different marbles we each had—their sizes and colors and how unusual they were made them all the more valuable in that lively conversation.

Not to be left out—and in my usual way of trying to fit in—I described a magnificent large steelie marble that I had in my collection. Mind you, all our marbles were safely out of sight at our homes, so bragging rights seemed like fair game to me.

Until that afternoon after school when there was a knock at our front door. I answered it—and there stood two of my schoolmates. When I saw them standing there I had a sinking feeling that something awful was about to happen. Instead of inviting them in, I stepped out on the porch to join them. Sure enough, they had come to see my magnificent marble. I just wanted to disappear. I had been found out and I had to admit it—out loud.

Worse than that was when my mother asked me what my friends had wanted. I confessed. Indeed, there are bragging rights and wrongs.

at Christmas tree

It seemed that little Gretchen wanted to play with her big brother's train instead of the doll and baby carriage she got that year. It was Christmas morning at our house with Mother (l to r) and me in Aunt Faye's lap and Uncle Herbert with my little brother Michael. My big brother Jan was happy with his train.

Christmas at Our House

When Christmas came around each year I could let my feelings show more. Others did, too. I loved those times.

The Christmas tree was in the front window when I was little and in later years it was at the other end of the living room between the windows that looked out at our mountains. Each year Daddy would take my brothers and me to pick out our Christmas tree at a local place that had brought them down from the mountains. We couldn't wait to get home and decorate the tree. It was a ritual to watch as Daddy and my big brother Jan unpacked the old-fashioned strings of colored lights and plugged them in—and circled them around the tree to the top where the star would shine the brightest. Then my little brother Michael and I would join in the decorating as we ever-so-carefully unwrapped the fragile hand-blown ornaments and put them on the branches we could reach. Last came the heavy box of old lead tinsel and we had to put it on one strand at a time so it would look like an icicle.

Family relatives would gather at our house on Christmas Eve, around the crackling fireplace, and we would sing carols and be happy to be together. Mother and Daddy always made sure to let the fire die down in time for Santa Claus to come down the chimney, and he always did!

Grandmother's house was next door and she would drape a string of those old-fashioned electric Christmas lights on her curtains at windows we could see from our house. Christmas brought our family even closer.

My mother had an electric candle lighted in the front hall window and it still shines in the darkness for me.

We grew up together—me and my dog Freckles were pals. We both had freckles marching across our noses.

My Most Memorable Christmas

It was my most memorable childhood Christmas. I went down the stairs from my bedroom and through the door into the living room—and my little girl's Christmas-morning-eyes saw him sitting over by the patio door.

My parents had gotten up in the dark to go get my little blond cocker spaniel puppy. There he was, waiting for me to pick him up and hold him tight and assure him that he had come home, just like I had come home all those years before when I was adopted.

And it didn't take long for me to know that my puppy came with a name—he had freckles marching across his nose just like me! We were inseparable that day and for days and years to come. Freckles was always there for me—and I didn't even have to use words for him to understand whatever it was that was going on inside of little-girl-me whenever I needed him.

# PART TWO: FINDING OUT

Bless her heart, my mother just couldn't part with my childhood things that I would bring home from school. I found this crayon picture in a box a lifetime later. The tablecloth was checkered red and white and the empty bowl reminded me of how it felt to be adopted. Even though I grew up in a loving family, being adopted was like there was an empty place inside me where I didn't know where I came from.

No Health History

I was living in Connecticut when it happened in the fall of 1985. I was a 48-year-old woman when I was diagnosed with breast cancer. That devastating news was made even worse because, since I was adopted, there was no biological health history for the doctors to go by. I had a mastectomy of my right breast that fall, and early detection was on my side.

It all came back to me, how my mother told me I was adopted—how I knew it was not to be talked about. I had lived my life just accepting that I didn't know where I came from. I had given up on ever knowing—until I had cancer. Cancer changes your life and cuts clear to the truth. I needed to know who my birth mother was. I needed to know my biological health history.

The next spring, I went back to my childhood home in Colorado Springs, to plead with my parents to help me find my birth mother. I pleaded and pleaded for their help, sobbing as I poured my heart out. I could feel their hearts hurting for me, but they said they couldn't help. The family doctor back then had made all the arrangements for the adoption—and he had died years ago. They couldn't help me.

While I was there with my parents that spring, Mother and I were sitting alone in her garden one morning—both of us expressing to each other how helpless we had felt about my breast cancer. It was then that I said to her, "All my life I have just been trying to find my way." With a longing in her voice that I will never forget, Mother said to me, "Some of us never do, honey." My heart hurt then when she said it, and it hurts again as I put these words on paper. Mother, you did find your way, your own way—let it be.

Before I left my hometown that spring, Mother and Daddy told me over and over again that they didn't know about my birth, that the family doctor took care of everything for the adoption. Someplace deep inside me didn't believe them.

Daddy's Dying Words

I didn't give up. Every so often I asked my parents on the phone if they would help me find my birth mother, and their answer was always the same—they were so sorry, they didn't know anything, and they couldn't help me.

It was March of 1992—and a telephone conversation with my father erased all time and distance. He was in a hospital in Colorado Springs, and I was a world away in Connecticut. Suddenly out of nowhere he said to me, "Honey, don't blame me for what I said, and don't blame me for what I didn't say." I was struck by his simple words that sounded like the confession of a dying man. The moment hung heavy with the truth. I knew at that moment that he knew. Everything inside of me knew that his disclosure was about where I came from. I silently took in what he had said and neither of us said any more about it. He had given me what I needed—the knowledge that there was something known where I had been told it was unknown.

My beloved father passed away hours later—as a new day dawned, as the sun came up across those vast plains and touched our mountains as it always did.

Daddy's revelation changed my life. Rather than continuing to ask Mother, "Will you help me find my birth mother?"—I changed my question to, "Have you considered telling me who my birth mother was?"

My Mother Told Me, Again

My name is Gretchen and I know where I came from because my mother told me.

It had been almost a year since my father died. As usual, I was talking with my mother long distance between Connecticut and Colorado. It was a Sunday afternoon in March of 1993.

As I had done before so many times in vain, I asked Mother if she had considered telling me who my birth mother was. There was a long silence, and then she said, "Have you been talking to Gingie?" "Was Gingie my birth mother?" "Yes, honey—but you can't tell anyone until after I have died."

How could she do that to me? How could she give me what I waited a lifetime to hear and then take it away from me, all in the same breath?

I had heard the most important words of my life and I couldn't have them—even then they weren't mine. They had to continue to be a secret, until Mother died. I couldn't even speak the truth about myself and where I came from. The fears of others continued to cloak the truth about me, about that adopted child that came to be named Gretchen.

What means the most to me is that my mother told me herself—in her own voice and words she revealed that Gingie was my birth mother. I cherish that moment. Everyone needs to know where they came from.

I learned along the way that Mother had told other family members about my birth mother—admonishing them, as well, not to let on until after her own death. Such was the spell of the secret of that secret named Gretchen.

It felt like my maternal grandmother next-door welcomed me into the family in this first photograph of me. Grandmother was holding me while my mother was looking at me. Grandfather Nipps was looking off in the distance, and my big brother Jan was presumably looking at our father taking the picture.

My first family portrait, in 1937.

With the help of a chair to lean on, little Gretchen learned how to stand on her own. Here I am at my Grandmother's house next-door.

A Different Reunion


After growing up as cousins in Colorado Springs, Gingie and I mostly just exchanged Christmas cards every year over the years.

Then in December of 1993, a Christmas card told me that Gingie and her husband Sam were going to be in Colorado Springs for the holidays. Even though my mother had warned me in March of that year never to tell anyone who my birth mother was until after she died, everything inside me said, "Go home and bring the truth out into the light with Gingie and Mother." Mother was in a nursing home then in my hometown.

The moment of truth was there for me. I had to call Gingie and tell her that I knew where I came from. I didn't know how she would react to my call, but I couldn't let myself think about it. She lived in Texas. I was at home in Connecticut. I had to call. But, it had been so long that the number I had wasn't her telephone number. I had to call the operator for help.

Finally, I dialed the number and felt my heart pounding as it rang.
She answered.
"Hi, Gingie—it's Gretchen." She seemed glad to hear my voice, and I said some "How's the weather?" words, or something, before jumping right into it.
"Gingie, I know you are my birth mother."
"Yes, I am."

Then there was a long-distance blur of emotions of relief and release for both of us. Most of all, I could tell that she wanted the truth out as much as I did. I had to take the final step before I could let myself think about it. We had a secret of our own—we planned that I would show up unexpectedly in Colorado Springs and we would go see my mother, her aunt, to tell her that the truth was out.

I was a bundle of mixed emotions when I boarded that plane in Connecticut, the day before the day of truth. I was scared of Mother's possible reaction and uncertain of how to relate to Gingie.

I arrived in Colorado Springs in the dark of night—I couldn't see my mountains. But, since they were always there for me, I could count on that and I needed them then, more than ever.
There I was in my hometown and all my relatives—except for Gingie and her husband—didn't know I was there.
I picked up the unfamiliar rental car and drove those familiar streets to the motel.
I couldn't sleep that night—I couldn't turn my mind off, as hard as I tried.
Then it came. The day finally came.

I went to see Gingie first. I didn't look up at her brother's house when I got out of that anonymous rental car and made my way up the sidewalk to the front steps— Gingie was there to welcome me with open arms and we cried.
There I was in Colorado, my birthplace in 1937.
There I was with Gingie, my favorite childhood cousin, my birth mother.
There I was with her brother's family—my family, too, of cousins and their children who were together for the holidays.
There I was to feel the shock on their faces when Gingie introduced me as her daughter, when we had been cousins all my life. I felt unsure about myself.
There I was amidst the relief and disbelief and joy as the truth came to light.

After an hour with Gingie and her family, it was time to go.
The time had come to take the truth to Mother, and Gingie went with me.

I was already overwhelmed with emotions as we got in the rental car to drive to the nursing home. Suddenly I was scared again about how Mother would react to what I'd done. Suddenly I feared it would be too much of a shock for her. Mother had a bad heart and what if she had a heart attack and it would be my fault? What if she disowned me and never spoke to me again? I questioned what I was doing—it all raced through my head—all the while trying to relate to Gingie, my cousin, my new-found birth mother in the seat next to me. I couldn't let myself think about it.

All I could do was drive and hold on to why I was there, to what had led me back to my homeland.

We arrived where Mother was and I parked that still-unfamiliar rental car.
I could tell Gingie was uneasy, too, as we walked into the building. We went to the front desk to identify ourselves and get directions to Mother's room. My heart was pounding as we neared the open door to her room—but she wasn't there!

We finally found where she was. I tried to walk ever so slowly and carefully to where she sat in a chair across the room. Gingie was several steps behind me. When I got to her, I knelt down to be close so she could see me, and I touched her with my hands to try to reassure her at that shocking moment.

"Mother, it's Gretchen, your daughter Gretchen."
She looked so confused.
I wanted to make it all better, I wanted it to be over.
"Mother, it's Gretchen and Gingie is here, too—when I heard she was coming for Christmas, I called her and told her that I knew she was my birth mother. I told her we would have a secret ourselves, that I would come unexpectedly and bring the truth out into the light."

The relief and release on Mother's face was palpable as it sunk in.
She squeezed my hands. "My Gretchen."
The truth was out. It was finally out.
By then others had gathered around us to witness what had happened.

The three of us went back to Mother's room, and I gave them the message I had hand-carried from Connecticut:

December 22, 1993

Dearest Mother, Dearest Virginia,

I have come to be with both of you in Colorado Springs this blessed
Christmas month of December 1993.
I have come to where my life began with both of you in Colorado in 1937.
I have come to be a part of our letting go of the dark secrets of my origin, as
we come together into the light of a circle come complete.
My heart is full to overflowing to have this connection come complete.
Dearest Mother, you are my Mother and you have been near to me along the
way, guiding and sustaining my life.
Dearest Virginia, you are my Birth Mother and you have been caring for me
from afar over the years.
I come carrying lighted candles in my heart for both of you, for giving me life
in so many ways.
I come believing there is rejoicing in the heavens as I say,
I belong to both of you.

With deepest gratitude and love forever,
Your Gretchen

More emotions on top of emotions overflowing.
Then I cried as Mother and Gingie thanked each other for Gretchen—Mother
thanked Gingie for giving birth to me, and Gingie thanked Mother for raising me
and making me her own.

What had been branded illegitimate was suddenly legitimate. Being legitimate is not
something someone can give or take away. It is a birthright, by being born—by
being born Gretchen in my family.

A circle had come complete—with Gingie (left) and me with my mother, her Aunt Billie. The truth was out.

My Birth Certificate

After the truth was out about where I came from, I longed to see my name and where I was born on the original certificate of my birth that had been filled out on June 23, 1937. I needed that tangible connection to my birth, to hold a copy of that legal document that said where I came from—where I really came from.

The official Colorado birth certificate that I had, that had been issued at my birth, didn't give a clue that I was adopted—my parents were my birth parents, or so implied. My place of birth was "Denver" and in the section indicated "Name of Hospital or Institution," it had "Hospital." The 1937 telephone book for Denver listed more than a dozen hospitals in the city then, and not one was named "Denver Hospital." The birth records of such secretive births as mine were meant to protect everyone from the truth.

I wanted to know the truth—and thankfully, both Mother and Gingie also wanted me to have a copy of my original birth certificate and encouraged me to get it. I started by making phone calls that led to more phone calls, and all the while I could sense the secrecy that hung over what I wanted.

I finally found where they could help me. Indeed, there were procedures to follow for such matters. They sent me forms to fill out and I carefully followed all the rules and regulations and submitted them, as instructed, by mail, in anticipation of seeing the truth of my origin.

Little did I know that the submission of those forms was the beginning of my trying to break through the system that had been set up to protect the secret of who I was, even from myself. It was like I was trying to find my way in a maze of bureaucratic red tape that led nowhere.

Those authorities didn't have the right to keep the truth from me—given that the truth was already out and I had been in the family all along. Mother and Gingie agreed with me and wanted to do whatever they could to help me get the copy of my original birth certificate. So the three of us wrote impassioned, notarized letters to those legal authorities who had been assigned our case. They couldn't help.

The secret of my birth had been sealed in secret forever. Or so it seemed. There I was in Connecticut—feeling helpless and a million miles away from where I was born, with no way to get to the truth. How could they withhold what was mine, my birthright? There had to be an answer, there had to be.

Who was the highest authority in the State of Colorado? There was the answer. After months and months of getting nowhere, I mailed a complete set of the documentation to the Office of the Governor of the State of Colorado—along with the photograph of the three of us on the day the truth came out. That material was then routed to the heads of the Citizens' Advocate Office and the Vital Records section of the Colorado Department of Health—and together they accomplished the outcome that we had been seeking for so long. They determined that there was no need to withhold a copy of my original birth certificate since all parties knew and affirmed my origin of birth and adoption—that my family of adoption was also my family of origin. The sealed file was opened and I received the certified copy of my original birth certificate.

There it was in someone's handwriting back then—I was born to be named Gretchen. My birth mother was named on the certificate, but not my birth father—so secrets still surrounded that part of the birth. Gingie had already told me that she couldn't remember who my birth father was. Nevertheless, I was holding it in my hands, the proof of where I was born—The Florence Crittenton Home in Denver.

The Florence Crittenton Home

I knew where I was born—The Florence Crittenton Home in Denver, Colorado. My original birth certificate had confirmed it in 1994. So, when I was making plans to go back to Colorado Springs for a summer visit three years later, I also wanted to arrange to drive to Denver to pay homage to my birthplace.

Once again the telephone made the long-distance connection to Colorado. When I tried to call The Florence Crittenton Home in Denver, I reached Human Services Inc. in Denver—a private, not-for-profit organization that had assumed The Florence Crittenton Home services in 1975.

I was told that The Florence Crittenton Home in Denver was founded in 1893, as a residential home for unwed mothers. I was born at that Home on June 23, 1937—and I hoped I could see it, and that there might be something in the records that documented my birth.

Alas, The Florence Crittenton Home no longer existed as it had been when I was born. And, unfortunately, most of the invaluable records from the Home had been destroyed. However, they still had the log books with the Admitted and Released dates of the girls who had lived at the Home—and they would look to see what they could find. Whatever the circumstances, I still longed to get as close as I could to where I was born. I made arrangements to meet with them when I was going to be in Colorado.

I was alone that morning and I had such a strong sense of expectancy as I drove to Denver—could it be that someplace deep inside me remembers my birth? I arrived at the address of the Human Services agency. They welcomed me warmly and it felt like they would help me. No one could have possibly understood my story better than they did. They knew about such matters. The Florence Crittenton Home had been called a safe place of "rescue" for pregnant teens and their babies. There I was, one of those babies born at the Home back in 1937. They understood.

The blessing was that they had found the entries and dates in the log books that documented my birth and adoption. They had taken the time and effort to carefully white-out all the other confidential information, so I could have photocopies of the pages that belonged to me:

"February 24, 1937—Martin, Rose Virginia, of Colorado Springs, was Admitted"
"June 23, 1937—Martin, Gretchen Louise, of Colorado Springs, was Born"
"August 7, 1937—Martin, Rose, of Colorado Springs, was Released to parents"
"September 1, 1937—Martin, Gretchen Louise, of Colorado Springs, was Released to Aunt who has adopted her today."

Gingie had told me that it was about two weeks after I was born when she went back home to Colorado Springs, and then her aunt and uncle drove to Denver to pick me up at The Florence Crittenton Home. One could only speculate why the truth was different from what she said. Why had she stayed at the Home so long after her baby was born? She couldn't remember. And why did my parents wait so long to go get me? There were no answers, only questions. Further, according to other records I had obtained, I was not legally adopted until May 31, 1938—again, for what reasons? I could only speculate.

At one point in the truth coming out, Mother said to me, "We always felt so steadily that you were ours." It surely had to take time before that baby would feel like their own. How could it not?

I will be grateful forever to the Human Services agency for assuming The Florence Crittenton Home services, so I could come home to myself.

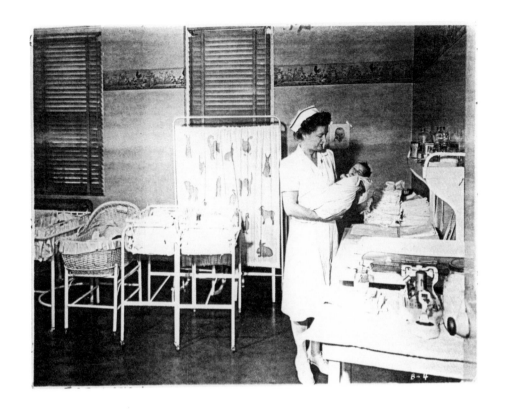

An early 1950s photograph from the archives of The Florence Crittenton Home in
Denver, where I was born. Perhaps little had changed from 1937.

What's in a Middle Name?

My middle name was Lee all my life. My name was Gretchen Lee vanHoosier. My middle name came from my father's middle name, Everett Lee. That was what was on my birth certificate all my life. That was all I knew my name to be, until I received a copy of my original birth certificate, and I saw for the first time: my name was Gretchen Louise Martin when I was born. Louise was my birth mother Gingie's mother's name, my mother's sister Louise, my favorite Aunt Weese.

Then, in further records that I obtained after the truth came out about where I came from, I learned that my parents had changed my name from Gretchen Louise to Gretchen Lee when they legally adopted me on May 31, 1938.

Did they change my middle name from Louise to Lee to remove any clue that could raise questions about my birth? Or was it to make me feel more like theirs with Daddy's middle name? Whatever the reasons, I belonged to all of them—and in my heart my middle initial "L" stands for both Louise and Lee.

The Year was 1937

June 23, 1937, was a Wednesday. On the day I was born, Eleanor Roosevelt was the First Lady of the land—I liked that.

On microfilm of *The New York Times* on my birthday, I found that the Rodgers & Hart's musical comedy hit, "Babes In Arms" was playing at the Shubert Theater and tickets were $1 to $3 for evening performances. TWA had the largest planes in America then, with the Lindbergh Line, and an automobile ad claimed that "the smartly styled new 1937 Studebaker had a wealth of wanted innovations." *The Times* cost two cents on my day of birth.

The average income in 1937 was $1,788. A new car cost $760 and a gallon of gas was ten cents. A loaf of bread cost a penny less. The life expectancy back in 1937 was 59.7 years.

On July 2, 1937, when I was ten days old, Amelia Earhart was lost at sea while on her round-the-world flight.

My hand is on my grandmother's knee, as if to be connected—I felt so sure of myself when I was close to her. My little brother Michael was there, too. This was our grandmother's house with her white wicker chairs on the lawn.

Grandmother's Letters

Along the way in writing this book, my dear cousin Bam sent me a box of letters that our grandmother had written back then—mostly to Bam's mother, my Aunt Lowell, my mother's sister and Grandmother's youngest daughter. The letters confirmed what I could only conjecture—how hard it was for my parents to adopt that baby. Grandmother was close by so she knew firsthand how it was. Grandmother was also the one who convinced them to adopt that baby.

Grandmother's letters didn't include this part, because it was a deep dark secret from everybody but those involved. But, with the truth out, Mother could tell me how her sister Louise had gone to their mother to plead for help to save her daughter Virginia's baby, so it wouldn't be lost forever. Louise also had to be pleading for the rescue of her first grandchild that she would never have that way.

It made no sense whatsoever that my parents would have taken on the burden to adopt that secret baby when my mother was in such poor health then—except that Grandmother had prevailed upon them that it was the right thing to do, to keep that baby in the family where it belonged. They adopted that baby named Gretchen and raised her as their own. They carried the burden of the secret and kept it secret to protect everybody.

One of the letters was written to Bam and her sister Margaret. Grandmother's own handwriting confirmed that she was the one who set the stage for that adoption in the family. The following were her words on May 19, 1937—the same time that her granddaughter Virginia was hidden away at The Florence Crittenton Home in Denver, waiting to give birth to that baby the next month, on June 23, 1937.

> "My own dear girls... Jan is doing very well in school, but he is just not crazy
> about going. He will be in the 1st grade next year for he will be six. Aunt
> Billie has always said she was going to adopt a baby when Jan was six.
> I wonder if she will..."

Grandmother knew to pose it as a possibility in her letter, so as not to give it away. She had set the stage for what was to come.

Secrets and Promises Kept

After the truth of where I came from was out in the open, I longed to know from
Gingie how it was when she got pregnant and I was born and who my birth father
was. I pleaded with her and she said she couldn't remember back then—except she
remembered holding her baby on a swing out on the lawn at The Florence
Crittenton Home where I was born, and she heard the popular song "Sweet Lai
Loni" off in the distance from a radio. I love knowing that.

In time I came to believe that what she said was the truth. Indeed, she couldn't
remember—she couldn't let herself break the promises that she had made to her
beloved mother and her grandmother and the aunt who adopted her baby. She told
me that they told her that all she was getting out of that baby was a cousin and
never to forget it. It was 1937, and that must have frightened an already scared
sixteen-year-old-girl into never telling what had to be kept secret forever.

The truth was she couldn't remember. I believe that even late in her life, even after
the deaths of all those who had threatened her, she could not speak, she could not
let herself speak, no matter how much she might have wanted to. The truth was she
couldn't remember. I believe she remembered deep inside herself, but she could
never let it come out. Alas, she did what she had promised them—and I would
never know what she alone knew about where I came from. Secrets still surround
that baby named Gretchen that was born back then. The fear of being struck by
lightning can come in many forms.

With the truth out, this became a very telling photograph from back then. Gingie, (far left) was as close as she could be to the one holding her baby, her cousin Gretchen. My parents were at the back (far right). Grandmother was in the center in her dark dress, with Aunt Weese, Gingie's mother, on one side and my big brother Jan on the other.

Secrets Beget Lies

I was taught to always tell the truth. When secrets are kept, they often have to be replaced with substitutes for the truth, whatever it was that was being kept secret. What are lies? The untruth? Something made up? And what if those untruths were made up to protect everyone? Are they bad then? When do they become lies?

What if the only way an illegitimate baby could be kept in the family was if it was kept in secret? What if everyone who kept the secret knew it was best for everyone? Do the best of intentions for all the right reasons make it right? When, if ever, do secrets turn into lies? Who decides?

Could circumstances justify the keeping of secrets? Could circumstances justify the keeping of lies to keep the secrets secret?

That baby that came to be named Gretchen would not have been adopted in that family if the truth had to be known. Secrets and lies were necessary to keep her in the family. They were protecting themselves and each other. They made a pact unto death—that they would keep the secret and take the secret to their graves—so nobody would ever know where that baby came from, for all the reasons they knew and for all the fears that bonded them together.

Two Mothers?

When the truth was out, she called me her daughter. What else would she call me if she was my birth mother? What else would she call me if she had waited all my life to call me that? I didn't know what to call myself in relation to Gingie. The truth was I didn't know how to relate to my birth mother. She was my cousin.

I called myself her daughter, too, even though I didn't feel differently towards her—except in my heartfelt knowing and gratitude forever that she gave birth to me. We exchanged mother-daughter cards to each other on birthdays and Christmas. I even sent her Mother's Day cards, but I never called her Mother. I always called her Gingie. That was who she was to me.

In time I came to realize that our needs were different about having the truth out about where I came from. I didn't need a birth mother. I needed to know who my birth mother was, to fill that void of unknown that was empty inside me. I already had a mother. Gingie needed to have her baby back that she had that she never had.

What they told her would never happen had happened. Emotionally, she had her baby back after a lifetime of longing—even though she knew in her mind that I was my mother's daughter.

I knew where I came from when the truth came out in December 1993, and I was blessed by that knowing. But it didn't change my life of who I was and how I was raised. Decisions were made back then, even before I was born in 1937, for how my life would be lived, who my relatives would be. We were raised as cousins.

I couldn't change my feelings. I tried. What was a birth mother supposed to feel like? What was a birth mother supposed to feel like when she was already your cousin all your life? How could you change a lifetime of feelings? I couldn't change my feelings. I had tried.

A Closing

My mother seemed to be playing "Hat" with her little niece named Virginia—
nicknamed Gingie.

My mother was born in 1902.
My cousin/birth mother Gingie was born in 1921.
I was born in 1937. My name is Gretchen.

May my words bring light where there was darkness, healing where loss and pain
have lingered, and may every page be blessed by the spirit of closure for what was
and what was not.

## The Book

The Book
is the place of pages,
one after one,
turned to reveal whatever was
and was not
to be revealed—
from what was
and what was not.

The Book
came to be
in a form
that could contain
whatever could be said,
or not—
of what one would say
about a journey.

The Book
could hold words
that would mark those places,
on pages,
where light prevailed
in the darkness—
where the unknown
came to be known.


Gretchen L. vanHoosier

ACKNOWLEDGMENTS

I AM GRATEFUL
to Agapita Judy Lopez, director of The Georgia O'Keeffe Foundation, in Abiquiu,
New Mexico, for her permission to use Georgia O'Keeffe's inspiring words,
"Making your unknown known—", from her 1923 letter to Sherwood Anderson.

I AM GRATEFUL
to all my family, known and unknown—here and beyond—who seemed to
accompany me in my writing of this story.

I AM GRATEFUL
to my beloved brothers, Jan and Michael, for encouraging me to tell my story my
way—affirming that we remember things differently from our growing up together.

I AM GRATEFUL
to all who helped me with my former notecards that taught me to trust my own
words, that opened the door to this book—especially those dear major contributors
who made that long journey possible: Gail and Jean Champlin, Debra Gold,
Lesley Schurmann, Jerry* and Paul Sciarra, Douglas* and Priscilla* Scott and
George* and Betty Pickering.
(*Bless them all—they passed away before I could give them my book.)

I AM GRATEFUL
to Kathy Ryan and the other generous ones who ever so patiently kept my copier
and fax machine going.

I AM GRATEFUL
to The Honorable Governor Roy Romer, State of Colorado, John Love of the
Governor's Citizens' Advocate Office, and Linda Eisnach, Chief of Vital Records,
Colorado Department of Public Health—who made it possible back in 1994 for
me to get a certified copy of my original 1937 Colorado Birth Certificate.

I AM GRATEFUL
to the kind and helpful staff of Human Services Inc. in Denver, Colorado—and
for permission to use the photograph from The Florence Crittenton Home archives.

I AM GRATEFUL
to Georgia Deoudes and others at The Evan B. Donaldson Adoption Institute in
New York City—for their pioneering work in improving the lives of people
touched by adoption.

I   A M   G R A T E F U L

to Richard Marold, the first and former director of the Cheyenne Mountain
Heritage Center and founder and former editor of its *KIVA* journal—for his
support, and encouragement to use the 1929 booklet (without a copyright notice)
titled, *Seedlet to Big Boy—An Impression of Cheyenne Mountain School* by writer
Farnsworth Crowder, the source of my kindergarten photograph.

I   A M   G R A T E F U L

to Leah Davis Witherow, archivist of the Starsmore Center for Local History of
the Colorado Springs Pioneers Museum—for permission to use the historical
photograph of my hometown streets of Colorado Springs, Colorado, when I was
growing up there.

I   A M   G R A T E F U L

to those select first readers of my manuscript who have blessed my words—
Gretchen Arnold, Susan Baker, Betty Anne Martin Crutcher, Lindsey Huddleston,
Cheryl Kloczko, Meg McMorrow, Lesley Schurmann, Pam Sottolano,
Sharon Vallone—and especially to Dorothy Mason and Jacqueline Germain,
who gave me light to go by all along the way.

I   A M   G R A T E F U L

to Robin Price, for her most skillful copyediting of my manuscript.

I   A M   G R A T E F U L

to Elizabeth Rose Campbell, for being my intuitive astrologer.

I   A M   G R A T E F U L

to Wil Altman, my computer guru with one foot in the stars, for bringing the
pieces of my book together in such a spirited way.

I   A M   G R A T E F U L

to Jack Meier, Abe Shamasian, Dave Caron and the many others who helped at
Connecticut River Press—for their attention to detail and carefully shepherding
my book into your hands.